Welcome to Canada

By Elma Schemenauer

The Child's World®

Published by The Child's World®
1980 Lookout Drive
Mankato, MN 56003-1705
800-599-READ
www.childsworld.com

Content Adviser: Dr. Andrew Nurse, Coordinator, Canadian Studies Academic Advisor
Programme, Department of History and Canadian Studies, Mount Allison University, Sackville,
New Bruinswick, Canada
Design and Production: The Creative Spark, San Juan Capistrano, CA
Editorial: Publisher's Diner, Wendy Mead, Greenwich, CT
Photo Research: Deborah Goodsite, Califon, NJ

Cover and title page: Keith Levit Photography/Index Stock Imagery, Inc.
Interior photos: Alamy: 4, (Worldspec/NASA), 7 (Dave Reede/AGStockUSA, Inc.), 18 (Robert
McGouey), 24 (Megapress), 26 (Tony Craddock/Images Etc. Ltd.); Corbis: 8 (Guenter Ziesler/zefa), 19
(Dan Lamont), 20 (Paul A. Souders), 27 (Brownie Harris); Getty Images: 3, 11 (Wayne R Bilenduke/
Stone), 22 (Joe McNally/Reportage), 25 (Gordon Wiltsie/National Geographic); iStockphoto.com: 28
(Ufuk Zivana), 29 (Walik), 30 (Tony Tremblay), 31 (Geoff Hardy); Minden Pictures: 9 (Mark Raycroft);
Mira.com: 6 (Brad Mitchell), 12, 17 (Andre Jenny); Oxford Scientific: 3, 15 (Diaphor La Phototheque);
Panos Pictures: 3, 14 (Alison Wright), 23 (Mark Henley); Landov: 13 (Reuters), 16 (Reuters/David
Ljunggren).
Map: XNR Productions: 5

Library of Congress Cataloging-in-Publication Data
Schemenauer, Elma.
  Welcome to Canada / by Elma Schemenauer.
     p. cm. — (Welcome to the world)
  Includes index.
  ISBN-13: 978-1-59296-911-1 (library bound : alk. paper)
  ISBN-10: 1-59296-911-9 (library bound : alk. paper)
  1. Canada—Juvenile literature. I. Title.

F1008.2.S 355 2007
971—dc22
                                2007005552

Contents

Where Is Canada? 4

The Land 7

Plants and Animals 8

Long Ago 10

Canada Today 12

The People 14

City Life and Country Life 17

Schools and Language 18

Work 21

Food 22

Pastimes 25

Holidays 27

Fast Facts About Canada 28

How Do You Say... 30

Glossary 31

Further Information 32

Index 32

Where Is Canada?

Imagine you are floating high above Earth. If you looked down on the planet, you would see some huge land areas surrounded by water. These land areas are called **continents**. Some continents are made up of several different countries. Canada is a huge country on the continent of North America.

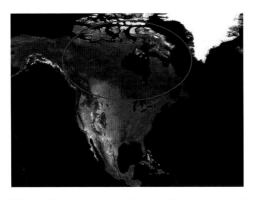

This picture provides a flat view of North America. Canada is located in and near the red oval.

Canada stretches from the Pacific Ocean to the Atlantic Ocean. Canada is so big that it is divided into ten smaller parts called **provinces**. Provinces are a lot like American states. Canada also has three areas called **territories**. Canada's territories are huge areas in the north of Canada.

Did you **know?**

Canada goes so far north that it almost reaches the North Pole!

4

ARCTIC OCEAN

GREENLAND

CANADA

⊛ National capital
★ Other capital
● Other city

N
W E
S

Baffin Bay

Alaska (U.S.)

Yukon

Northwest Territories

Nunavut

★ Iqaluit

Labrador Sea

Whitehorse ★

★ Yellowknife

Newfoundland and Labrador

Hudson Bay

St. John's ★

British Columbia

Alberta

Saskatchewan

Manitoba

Quebec

Edmonton ★

Prince Edward Island

Nova Scotia

Vancouver ●

Calgary ●

Ontario

Charlottetown ★

Fredericton

Victoria

Regina ★

Quebec ★

Halifax ★

Winnipeg ★

New Brunswick

Montreal ●

Ottawa ⊛

ATLANTIC OCEAN

Toronto ●

UNITED STATES

0   200   400 miles

0   200   400 kilometers

Banff National Park in Alberta

The Land

A farmer and his son look at their fields in Manitoba.

Since Canada is so big, there are many different kinds of land. Western Canada has many beautiful mountains. The Atlantic region is covered with grassy hills. Huge fields of crops stretch across Canada's Prairie Provinces—Alberta, Saskatchewan, and Manitoba. In the Eastern Lowlands, the weather is warm enough to grow apples and peaches.

Another land area in Canada is called the Canadian Shield. Very few people live in this area because it is rocky and cold. In Canada's far north, it is windy and frozen most of the time. That's because the North Pole isn't very far away!

Did you know?

Mount Logan in the Yukon Territory is the highest mountain in all of Canada. It stands 19,551 feet (5,959 meters) tall.

7

Bighorn sheep can be found in mountain areas.

Plants and Animals

Each area of Canada has its own kinds of plants and animals. Gophers and badgers live in the huge fields of the Prairie Provinces. In the Eastern Lowlands, hawks and owls soar high above the trees. The tall grasses of the Atlantic region are home to many rabbits and deer. Bighorn sheep live high in the mountain areas. And the beautiful Canadian Shield has thick forests that hide moose and bear.

The animals that live in Canada's far north have bodies that are specially made for living in cold temperatures. Polar bears have thick fur to keep them warm. And seals have a thick layer of fat that protects them from freezing weather.

Did you know?

Canada is also home to several kinds of animals that are in danger of dying out. Some of them can only be found in Canada, such as the Newfoundland marten and the Vancouver Island marmot. Scientists and others are working to save these animals.

A black bear

Long Ago

The first people came to Canada thousands of years ago. Today, Canadians refer to these people as "First Nations" and **Inuit** (IN-yoo-it). Many different First Nations have lived in parts of Canada for a long time. Some groups, such as the **Cree** (KREE) people, now live in Ontario, Québec, and western Canada. The Inuit live across the Canadian north. In the past, these people hunted animals and farmed the land.

Over the years, other people moved to Canada. People from France and Great Britain came in the 1500s and 1600s. They brought new languages and ways of life to Canada. But they also forced many native people off the land where they had lived for generations.

An Inuit man and his dog team take a rest by an igloo.

Canada Today

Today, the people of Canada try to share the land, but sometimes there are problems. Sometimes First Nations people and the other Canadians disagree about who owns the land. Still they all work to live together peacefully despite their differences.

People visit the shops and restaurants on a narrow street in Québec City.

A group of people who want Québec to stay a part of Canada gather in Calgary.

Sometimes English- and French-speaking Canadians have problems, too. The province of Québec (kwuh-BEK) or (ki-BEK) is different from other Canadian provinces. Most people in Québec speak French and most people speak mainly English in the other areas. Some of the people in Québec want their province to be a country of its own. Most of the other residents in Québec, however, want Canada to stay together.

13

The People

More than 31 million people live in Canada's provinces. Most of them live in the southern part of the country, where the temperatures are warmer. About one-third of all the people in Canada live in the province of Ontario. After Ontario, the largest Canadian provinces are Québec and British Columbia.

Three Inuit children play on a swing on Baffin Island.

Just like Americans, Canadians come from different backgrounds. Many Canadians have British or French backgrounds. Others have relatives that came from places such as Asia, Africa, Latin America, and the Caribbean.

Canada's native peoples are only a small part of Canada's population. But they are growing fast. Nearly 1 million Canadians have native **ancestry**.

An outdoor market in Toronto

In the Canadian Arctic, many people use snowmobiles to get around.

City Life and Country Life

Diners enjoy a meal outside at a cafe in Québec City.

Life in Canada is very much like life in the United States. In the cities, people live in apartments or houses. They drive their cars or take the bus.

People can shop in supermarkets and shopping malls. In Canada's countryside, people live in houses just like ours. They drive their cars from place to place. Roads are good, and there are many small towns.

In Canada's far north, life is very different. In the winter many roads are too rocky and rough for cars. Instead, some people use snowmobiles to go places. Where there aren't roads, people use airplanes and boats to move around. Some people even travel by dogsled in the far north. Mostly, though, dogsleds are used for fun or for racing.

Schools and Language

Canadian schools are much like American schools. Children start kindergarten when they are about five years old. They learn reading, writing, and math. Students also study science, social studies, and music, just as you do. Many Canadian children also learn how to use computers.

In many parts of Canada, signs are written in English and French.

English and French are both official languages in Canada. All Canadians learn at least a little bit of each language in school. In Québec, students spend more time on French since that's the province's main language. In New Brunswick, both languages are important since a lot of people there speak English and French. In parts of Canada, road signs must be written in both languages for everyone to understand them.

A student examines an animal skull during class.

Loggers take down trees in a forest in British Columbia.

Work

There are many kinds of jobs in Canada. In the cities, many people work in offices, factories, and stores. In the countryside, farmers grow crops and raise animals.

Loggers cut trees from the forests to make paper and buildings. Along the seashore, people sell fish, lobsters, and clams. In the far north, people hunt, fish, and trap animals for their furs.

Did you know?

Canadians call their dollar coins "loonies."
That's because the coin has a bird called
a loon on the back.

Food

Canadians eat lots of different foods. Supermarkets in Canada have everything from microwave dinners to canned soups. Many Canadians still eat dishes their long-ago relatives, or ancestors, enjoyed. They eat corn and beans like some of the First Nations people. They make pea soup like the early French settlers. And they eat beef and drink tea like the early British

A waitress carries food for customers at a restaurant in Vancouver.

Shoppers check out the fresh tomatoes offered at this market stall.

settlers. Canadians also eat plenty of foods brought by
newer settlers. Restaurants in Canada serve everything
from Italian pasta to Chinese egg rolls.

A group of children play ice hockey,
one of Canada's most popular sports.

Pastimes

Because much of the country has long, cold winters, Canadians play many winter sports. Children slide down snow-covered hills on long sleds called **toboggans**. Children in Canada also like to snowshoe, ski, skate, and play ice hockey—just like American kids! In summer, children like bike riding, roller skating, and swimming. Soccer, baseball, football, lacrosse, and basketball are popular team sports. Many families like to camp in Canada's beautiful mountains and countryside. And for those who like the city, there are plenty of shows to see and museums to visit.

A mother and son celebrate their big catch at one of Canada's many lakes.

Did you know?

Canada has more than 40 national parks where people can go hiking, camping, fishing, and more.

Brilliant fireworks fill the night sky at Niagara Falls to celebrate Canada Day.

Holidays

Crowds gather at the Skydome in Toronto to watch a baseball game.

Canadians and Americans have many of the same holidays. Both countries celebrate Christmas, New Year's, and Halloween. Canadians celebrate their country's birthday, too. On Canada Day, July 1, people fly Canada's red-and-white maple-leaf flag. They hold parades and picnics, and shoot off fireworks. Canada Day is a lot like the Fourth of July in the United States.

Canada is a huge country with many special things to see and do. Maybe one day you will visit Toronto's Skydome to watch the Blue Jays baseball team. Or perhaps you'll go to see the giant stuffed frog near the city of Fredericton. Or maybe you'll watch a white shaggy polar bear roam across the arctic ice. Wherever you go, Canada is sure to be an interesting place!

27

Fast Facts About Canada

Area: 3,855,000 square miles (9,984,670 square kilometers). This is a little larger than the United States.

Population: More than 31 million people.

Capital City: Ottawa.

Head of Government: The prime minister.

Head of State: Queen Elizabeth II and her representative, the governor general.

Other Important Cities: Toronto, Montreal, Vancouver, and Edmonton.

Money: A Canadian dollar is divided into 100 cents.

National Flag: A red and white flag with a red maple leaf in the center. The maple leaf is Canada's national symbol.

National Animal: The beaver.

National Holiday: Canada Day on July 1. Canada Day is a lot like the Fourth of July in the United States.

National Colors: Red and white.

National Song: "O Canada."

O Canada!
Our home and native land!
True patriot love in all thy sons
    command.
With glowing hearts we see thee rise,
The True North strong and free!
From far and wide,
O Canada, we stand on guard for thee.
God keep our land glorious and free!
O Canada, we stand on guard for thee.
O Canada, we stand on guard for thee.

Famous People:

Margaret Atwood: author

Frederick Banting: Nobel Prize-winning scientist

Roberta Bondar: first Canadian woman in space

Tommy Douglas: politician, founder of the country's medicare system

Wayne Gretzky: professional ice hockey player

Sir John A. Macdonald: first prime minister of Canada

Michael Ondaatje: author

Lester B. Pearson: prime minister, Nobel Peace Prize winner

David Suzuki: scientist, author, and television host

Pierre Trudeau: prime minister, politician

Canadian Folklore:

In 1535, an explorer got lost and two native children told the explorer about a village that was close by. The word in their language was "kanata." When the explorer got back to his friends, he told them about the land he had visited—only he called it "Canada," instead. That is how Canada got its name!

How Do You Say...

ENGLISH	FRENCH	HOW TO SAY IT
hello	bonjour	boh-ZSHOOR
goodbye	au revoir	oh rah-VWAHR
please	s'il vous plaît	seel VOO play
thank you	merci	mer-SEE
one	un	UNH
two	deux	DOO
three	trois	TWAH
Canada	Canada	CAH-nah-dah
Québec	Québec	kwuh-BEK

Glossary

ancestry (ANN-ses-tree) Ancestry means that a person has ancestors, or relatives from long ago. The ancestors of many Canadians came from places like Asia and Europe.

continents (KON-tuh-nents) Most of the land areas on Earth are in huge sections called continents. Canada is on the continent of North America.

Cree (KREE) One of Canada's native peoples who live in Ontario, Quebec, and western Canada.

Inuit (IN-yoo-it) One of Canada's native peoples who live in the northern part of Canada.

provinces (PRO-vin-sez) Canada is divided into ten smaller sections called provinces.

territories (TARE-uh-tor-eez) Canada's territories are huge areas in the north of Canada.

toboggans (tuh-BAH-gunz) Toboggans are long sleds that are curved up at one end. Many toboggans are made of thin pieces of wood, but some are made from metal or plastic.

Further Information

Read It

Bowers, Vivien. *Only in Canada!* Toronto: Maple Tree Press, Inc., 2002.

Braun, Eric. *Canada in Pictures.* Minneapolis, MN: Lerner Publications Co., 2003.

Landau, Elaine. *Canada.* Danbury, CT: Children's Press, 2000.

Look It Up

Visit our Web page for lots of links about Canada:
http://www.childsworld.com/links

Note to Parents, Teachers, and Librarians: We routinely verify our Web links to make sure they are safe, active sites—so encourage your readers to check them out!

Index

animals, 8–9
area, 28
British Columbia, 14
Canadian Shield, 7, 9
capital city, 28
education, 18
farming, 7, 21
flag, 28
food, 22–23
government, 13
history, 10
industries, 21
landforms, 4, 7
landmarks, 27
language, 13, 18
major cities, 28
money, 21, 28
national holidays, 27, 28
national song, 28
native people, 10, 12, 14
natural resources, 7, 21
New Brunswick, 18
places of interest, 7, 13, 14, 18, 27
population, 14, 28
Quebéc, 10, 13, 14, 18
sports, 25
Toronto, 27
weather, 7